Full Nova

Full Nova

CALEY O'DWYER

Orchises
Washington
2001

Library of Congress Cataloging-in-Publication Data

O'Dwyer, Caley, 1970-
  Full Nova / Caley O'Dwyer
  p. cm.
  ISBN 0-914061-85-2 (alk. paper)
  I. Title

    PS3565.D66 F85 2001
  811'.6-dc — 21   00-039154

··

ACKNOWLEDGMENTS

Grateful acknowledgment is made to the following publications in which some of
these poems first appeared: *Faultline, Hayden's Ferry Review, Many Mountains
Moving, Poet Lore, The Quarterly, River Oak Review, Santa Barbara Review, The Sarah
Lawrence Review, Spelunker Flophouse, Tex, The Texas Review, Thorny Locust, UCI
Journal, Washington Square*, and *Xanadu*.

Thanks also to the Helene Wurlitzer Foundation for support during the period in
which some of these poems were written.

In addition, the author wishes to extend his gratitude to Jac Alder, Edward
Anhalt, Tom Babayan, Allison Benis, Mila Drumke, Hugh Feagin, Beth Henley,
Thomas Lux, James McMichael, Jeredith Merrin, Larry O'Dwyer, Michael Ryan,
and Edward Swift.

··

Manufactured in the United States of America

Orchises Press
P.O. Box 20602
Alexandria
Virginia
22320-1602

G6E4C2A

for

Camilla Carr

CONTENTS

AFTERWARD

First there are the sands.
There is the sea and the sound of wind.
You live, and it is in this corridor
that you remember. This narrow passage
between the whitewash and palms
is where you become.
Gulls sweep endlessly to the north.
They are what you know of travel. Sure
wayfarers of time, they glide
and age. From your perspective
there is no summer, though you know
that's where they are heading, even
through the pale winter light you can barely see
beyond language. You know
what you were born to do, and see how stars
accomplish fire at nightfall.
One day you will wake and hear
no wind, no ocean. You will hear,
white sands, still palm, blue heron, the letters
of each word traveling from you, like the gulls
flying in groups up the remembered coast.

YELLOW COREOPSIS

It was the idea of fishing that I liked.
Not the act of fishing, but the thought of casting
the weighted line, the high arc
before it sunk. The slow unraveling.
Mostly, waiting was dull
but I liked watching the bob
lazy on water, green
fold-out chairs surrounded
by beer cans and branches
and my Grandfather saying, "Well, Kelly,
I guess we're havin' a good time."
Small dead trout floated at the top of the fish canister.
Ones that lived balanced at the bottom,
and I could smell the sour breath of water
through large airholes where they were fed.
When we got home, ones that swam we fried.
Dead ones were buried, and months later,
bloomed in the yard: slender, bright
coreopsis. To see them
knowing they were made of scales, gills, eyes, fins,
we had dragged, living,
from water. To reach down,
touch the stems. To smell
with all I knew of ends, large cups
unfolding yellow.

ICE VICTIM AT LAKE WINNIPEG

When my heart stopped, they say
the ice turned black. Under-water
rose where the landscape had been cracked
to an arctic shudder. The green coat
bobbed on its back until the body bobbed over.
The newspaper read, *Collarbone*
Hooked On Loose Drainpipe. They say
it's what saved me. What had been held inside
was let go, and for a moment
glass brightened on the water.
Winters are so cold with dry wind and frost
over nature. Shadow in a cave
then light opening toward the river.
Under the deep brace of ice
when my eyes opened and the heart
began again under the rib bones,
I imagine they felt what ice must feel
when summer comes and thaws all cold
back into river. I was nine.
Windows brightened on the mountain, birds
flashed in the limbs. What absence
did I enter, as the day-owl's cry spread
down the lifeline? Others were looking in,
and those who knew the face watched as it changed
in the white branches.
I hear them calling in the night.
The sound is ash, or fingers opening.

DON'T LOOK IN THE LAKE BOAT

Don't look in the lake boat. If you look
you will turn to a pillar
of salt. Look

and it will be done for you
what was done to the one
in the lake boat.

It is dark.
In a wood without leaves
the wind is swaying its empty star.

If you follow me to the lake water
where the lamplight is orange
and yellow on the stones,

if you drink the water,
if you smoke,
if you drink the water

out of the broken boat,
do not ask what I have done.
Do not ask about the lake boat.

In the summers I do not work.
It is summer,
do not look.

And yet you are right,
it is late, and what is there
could change and may, behind your back,

become your life. We must check.
Come with me to the lake water.
But don't look back.

PLASTIC LILIES

I

It's not the tower that's Big Ben, nor is it the clock.
It's the bell.

It's one candelabrum, two or more candelabra.

Brides don't walk down the aisle, they walk down the nave.

Speakers don't stand behind a podium, they stand behind
a lectern.

The Hundred Years War lasted a hundred and sixteen years.

It's Neptune, not Pluto, that's farthest from the sun.

No witches were burned in Salem.

Bamboo is a grass.

II

Leaves have meaning.
No. Leaves do not have meaning.

Signs have meaning.
What is a sign?

A sign refers to something that has meaning.
Then the something has meaning, not the sign.

If the sign were a symbol, could it have meaning?
Can a symbol be a sign?

III

The self is a place where signs join.
What if the signs do not join?

Think of cousin Betty.
Yes.

IV

How are the crops, the wife, the kids, the couch, the vegetable?
How is the portrait, the office, the medal, the savings, the bank?

How is the future?

15

What was the past.

What are you thinking?
I'm thinking of the way you think of me.

Cousin Betty is very sick.
She's dead.

Lilies grow in the yard.
They are plastic.

Nonetheless, lilies they are.

GOLDFISH

The bodies of the pond lilies only look awake
in the winter, green backs not yet gray,
and the limp structure of leaf flesh, which
dives down into stopped water
that wishes it were rain,
is frozen tight into a glass casing
over the pond's clear face.
And despite warming light
looking into the surface for life,
there is no leaf nor living thing
in the stop-time underworld to wake.
But there, under the ruined pond's forehead,
in full red, a goldfish, like a thought,
a quick streak of blood in the mind's vein.

FULL NOVA

In the school yard they are gathering.
They call your name across the field.
Dave's got the ball.
All day you've been trapped in the gloom

of World History. Ice men
forged sharpened flint to fiber rope,
precursor to the knife. Rufus
busted open Henry II's English castle

and fire is the result of rubbing. Ned says
hike, and soon it's in your hands.
You're back in shotgun, blitz
oncoming, Bobby Rearden's little brother

rushing head-on with scrawny white arms,
front line breaking up, arm cocked and
following till the fingers let go and you're
face down in a puddle of mud.

2nd and 10. 1210 is the year Eric X
stormed Sverker II, King of Sweden, and that August,
the creation of a machine for spinning flax.
Shakespeare was a dramatist—remember, Romeo

died, Juliet insisted. Snap.
Hand off to Hillman, who goes wide,
poking back his defender, a fattened
Polish boy who speaks little English

and can't play much football either.
Poland is a country in middle Europe,
also the brand name of butter.
Hillman gets up, distressed. Wasn't

someone supposed to help him? No,
and lunchtime's waning. At 3rd and 4
passing might not be the best option,
so you begin to shovel back,

but no one's there. Catherine De Medici,
Queen Consort to France, was alone, too,
when she made a poor decision.
You run straight through the middle

brushing spears and long swords to the side,
head to head with a Trojan battle ram,
deus ex machina, Todd Holbert and his
mouth full of shiny silver braces.

First down. The appearance of Perseus
in the northern constellations, 802.
Plants are green because of chlorophyll.
Thomas Edison is responsible

for lightbulbs. Or was it telephones? Quick
fake handoff to left, wide out
to line of scrimmage, and Monty
catches your lousy toss

for a twenty-nine-yard gain into the rain shower
at the fifty-yard line. You rush downfield,
closer to the soccer posts and Jenny Lupit,
her new tennis shoes and freckles

dazzling like Andromeda. Why should it matter
who killed who when Jenny Lupit's lips
are red as mom's garden wheelbarrow?
She likes the planets, but how much

will you have to learn and say before she says
yes? Would you trade a year of sack lunches
for a single kiss? Full nova,
Mr. Glasser suggests, is a star

that increases its light output
suddenly, a tremendous euphoria, and then
fades in a few months or years
into obscurity. Touchdown

if you can hit Berry three feet from the end zone,
but that guy who keeps sniffing glue and
rolling up glueballs in 3rd period
blocks him out, and it's 2nd and half a century.

PHOTO WITH SNAIL SHELL

I'm holding up a snail shell
to show you what happens
when we don't speak. I go
inside, and the walls
of what I understand
narrow. Behind, the fir tree
might have swayed,
or was it not a cool day,
quiet? Other trees,
starker, a lamppost
at the point where sidewalk
fades. We could look at
what happened, but there's
nothing beyond this yard. There is no
other light in the world
but what you see,
blurred behind the small figure
looking out at you. What's ahead
is you, looking in at me.

SNAKE

The endlessness of scales and the body. If you
follow contour, shape
swallows existence. Its tongue,
pointed fire, says *this, this, this*
(desire to touch and kiss), and
thus death is a life
entering its mouth.
In its body, a body breaks.
Pink ears go dark in acid.
In trees, birds tell each other how they heard
pleasure just before the mouse
entered (that need
to point out what is there before it's
taken). The cricket waits for this to pass,
knowing its last taste may be
itself devoured. Thin heat
slides forward as if time were
no matter. White flowers
bend in the field.
The cricket feels its life
open. A slither in the grass. The body
flashes past, stops where its future is the end
of one, small, disconsolate creature. A field mouse
frightens itself to sleep in the mouth of its speaker.

HE CLICKS AND WAITS

She will come.
A black night's end
shows its least star

glowing. Back legs
strum and red eyes
fear pleasure.

She is feeling her way
through error:
a forewing

wedged in a groove of dirt,
white twigs braced
against her. Grass

is erotic, bending
and unfolding in the field. Frogs
make low music

between reeds. He repeats
the highest note
on his body. She will

drain him. It kills him
to feel her
approaching. Snow

would be better.
It is dying, this
hot work to touch her.

A LUNA MOTH SAILS THROUGH THE NIGHT

And the cricket feels it is there,
seeing its shape appear
green against the cold
blue stars. It is what the cricket
wishes to feel: swift,
continuous passage. Wind
shudders the grass.
There is a difference between the sun
and this light that lives: the sun can't see
the cricket watching in the fields.
Streams of wide blue move like water
in the sky. When the cricket
makes its dry music it's because
there's nothing else
to feel. But the luna moth
makes its silence
echo in the field.

CHILLICOTHE

I

In Chillicothe,
everyone waves,
and no one reads

The Waste Land.
Food is good,
and grass and pecans

grow there,
and chickens caw out
from wire cages

in the one-hundred-and-five-degree sun.
There is one school, one bank
and one policeman.

Arriving there, you will find
people on porch steps
waiting for tornadoes.

II

Crunching inexpensive gravel,
the engine whinnies out
like a fat man off to nap.

The guest looks out the passenger window
and, being his only passenger,
rolls it up

so that horseflies don't eat
the vinyl seats and shit
on the dashboard.

When the swing door
springs open
the host pops out,

her eighty-year-old face
wrinkled as a newborn
pigeon, all veins and warbly eyes.

III

The Funeral parlor
provides the town's
greatest source of income.

Everyone dies,
and most people
are old.

The woman who arranges
the burials
depends on it.

Her family
was born
out of a town full of dying,

and a womb
under a plump belly.
It still jiggles like cold jelly.

IV

The old lady
snores like cicadas
in her recliner,

dreaming of better days.
She is not dead.
Her toes are pink

and twitch
when the dreams are good.
In fifteen minutes

she will awaken
to wash dishes
and eat ice cream.

Her eyes jitter at the lids.
Fireflies are stars behind her.
They glow, then disappear in the wind.

V

Why does he try
to stop
loving her so much

when she is going off to sleep
for maybe the last time?
He cannot care, and dreams

of baseball games and wisteria bushes
in her hair. In the morning
she is mixing up

pancake batter, wondering
did he get any sleep, does he want breakfast,
handing him the orange juice pitcher

and sixteen pieces
of greasy bacon with toast
beside a thick lump of melting butter.

VI

When will she go,
the tall reclining lady
in the electric adjustable chair,

and yellow corn for teeth
and eyes that no longer care;
when will she go,

through the cigarette smoke
and the swing door
that slams of visitors

that don't come back anymore;
when will she go,
with bony callused feet

through teeth of unmowed grass
and pecans that won't be cracked;
when will she go

to the drying lines out back
to pin up the last wet load
of summer laundry?

VII

"I never seen anything like it.
Next he'll wear his underpants
and baptize Jewish babies," she says,

returning from church,
complaining that the new pastor
is gay,

maybe. In the mirror she sees
that her hair will fall apart,
held together only by starch

from the hairdresser's spray can.
Everything is brittle in a town like this.
All of its photographs

and dishes have cracks.
Some of its citizens
have plastic kneecaps.

VIII

The lady with a cobweb face
was bit by three dogs
three times in her life

and mows her lawn
across the street
like a sculptor.

She does not go out
on the trips to Vernon
for country-fried steak. She stays home

and cooks green beans
with tuna-rice casserole, occasionally
sewing patches

in family quilts.
She lives alone
and dislikes children.

IX

In the daytime the guest
searches in the brush
out back of the house

for cattle bones
at hush
near vacant trains.

At night he holds
an eye socket
to the moon

letting light
flow through
into her dreams.

He cups the bones
between his palms
and briefly sings.

X

The Plymouth wakes in the carport
like a loud man getting up.
The wheels back it slowly out,

staying clear of lemongrass
where the water ditch
drops a foot.

The guest waves good-bye,
glancing for cars to the left,
and the little old woman

on wooden knees
enters the sunlight,
coming forward

from the carport, into sunlight,
as the whole car disappears
into the trees.

HOW I LEFT MICHIGAN

Every day,
the wind picked up and let out the snow.

Once, it took my sheets
and shirts

into the clouds. I followed them to Nebraska.
Sure, there was nothing there either,

and the people few
and oddly shaped —

I liked the way it felt
to dislike it there.

RADISHES IN BELL JARS

Our galaxy moves quickly
in the wrong direction. At 1.56
million miles per hour, or four hundred thirty-five
per second, every planet
from earth out to a span of six million light-years on all sides
is being carried toward some distant point
beyond Orion. You're sitting in a rowboat
rowing hard toward friends you see ahead, also rowing.

On one side you see you're closing in fast on some rocks
lining an embankment. As you row toward friends, you're also
carried downstream. Your net motion is the sum of both, and it's
across the river, toward the rocks.
Hundreds of galaxies are caught, each with local motion,
yet all are taken toward a place
where the afterglow of the Big Bang is ever so
slightly hotter, bluer, shorter.

When Penny Boston saw no giraffes, shrubs or even
weeds in those dead pictures from Mars, she set out
trying to grow some life-forms. Difficult to believe
there would be nothing to look for on a planet whose
average temperature is only thirty-eight degrees
colder than our own, and whose days, despite
double-long revolutions around the sun, are a mere
forty-two minutes longer.

Things died in the jars.
Radishes, cockroaches, bananas. She tried
creating the exact composition of martian soil
but live specimens, even hybrid,
flattened. The one element entirely
missing from martian soil is what the term
organic chemistry is based on.
Minus carbon, things don't live.

DEAD CANARY

I saved the bird you loved.
It's in the closet under the stool.
I should have fed it more often,
but the longer you stayed away
the more your absence
distracted my attention.

Still, its eyes have that
open quality
the live bird had,
and when you prop it up on the mantle
above the stove, it looks so happy
you'd think it could fly.

Also, the grass died,
and the jonquil, the two fish
in the bottle and the potato in the jar
over the windowsill.
The cat had only one life,
remains of which are neatly folded
under the porch.
The tire swing, full of rope,
no longer hangs from the tree.

Did you think you could leave me so long
to water nettle and pluck

dead lacinula from the shrubbery?
I have waited here only to tell you
the foundation of this house
is unstable. You can see
by girders hanging in the window,
this house is ready to fall.

BETTY

Betty's got a brass boat over a glass flat coat.
She's got a kid full of snot
and an awful lot of money.

Betty's got Bill, but Bill's got Eddie.
Eddie's got a truck, and that ain't much.
Bill's got a problem and he calls it Betty.

Eddie's in the bed with Bill right now.
Bill's in the bed with Eddie.
Poor Betty.

Betty's a baby when it comes to Bill.
Bill's limp when it comes to Betty.
But not when it comes to Eddie.

Betty is bright, but she's not too smart.
She's got a gouging wound of an open heart.
She's got a ring and an "I do" and a document.

Betty is pretty and tall and straight.
Betty is something Eddie would eat.
But Bill will do.

Still, Eddie's not sure if Bill's the true Mc Q.
He'll do all right for a lifetime though.
He'll do OK for a lifetime.

Betty bought Bill an African float
so he can go down the Nile
in a tailcoat.

Bill bought Eddie a brand-new truck.
And that ain't much. Eddie smiled and said,
"just my luck."

But you should have seen what Eddie got Betty.
You should have seen how thick and huge.
You should have seen what Betty did to Eddie

after she said to Bill, "I'm through."
"I'm through," she said to Bill,
"I've had quite enough of you."

Now Bill is alone and doesn't like either.
Bill is alone and that's OK.
Bill doesn't like anyone anyway.

Now Eddie's got Betty and Betty's got sex.
Betty's got Eddie's
Tyrannosaurus Rex.

Go Betty!
And there she is on top of Eddie. Out pops
another baby.

Eddie's got a brass boat over a glass flat coat.
He's got two kids full of snot
and twice as much money.

Betty's got Eddie who's got a very large prick.
Betty's got Eddie who's got nothing to say.
Eddie's got a grandkid for his daddy who's sick.

"Look," one day I hear him say, "I don't like Betty,
she's not for me, and why I fuck her
is a mystery.

She'll do all right for a lifetime though.
She'll do OK for a lifetime."

TRIO

As Harold Saw It

Tom was a different man, so common
and reasonably content with the Laundromat
and such elements as "the relationship,"
frequent talk of getting a bigger dog and new silverware,
maybe a TV and/or a cat—

but I am extremely aware of the fact
that Tom's life was not progressing
and was making him latently upset,
for even when Tom was promoted
to manager of the dry cleaning building,
his left eye still drooped,
and the occasional violent angle
in his right pupil remained like the too extant knife
hooked into a dead man's throat.

One night, motoring in Letty's father's yacht,
I caught Tom preparing a delicate dish of strawberry crepes,
folding the layers of each dessert
as sleeves and shoulders of a freshly cleaned shirt,
glancing at intervals between sweet and sweet
to note the mild burning at both bony feet
where the portable stove urged its light.
He stopped momentarily to eat.

As the boat swayed, his eyes rocked.
He clasped the knife and stroked
the fat of his belly, which jiggled
precisely as jelly jiggles when touched.
That was it. He had the look.
His wide fleshy fingers slid along the blade,
blue and purple veins pressing at the tip.
How slowly the uncanny smile crawled out.

I watched him from the upper deck.
Letty slept in the sleeper.
It was two o'clock. He sat in the lawn chair and gazed,
eating strawberries. The clock struck its warning. The knife
slipped into the butter dish. The red peppers were cooked.
He walked to the counter and released
the peppers from the oven. His left eye sank.

Letty's voice called out,
Hey, Tom, you shit, I'm hungry.
Mechanically, monomaniacally,
Tom prepared the last garnishes of lunch.
The napkins were delicately folded.
Gathering the angles of his eyes,
and in his arms the butter and peppers,
he proceeded knife first into the hall,
down the stairs into the sleeper,
where Letty sprawled like dirty laundry.

He smiled big. His teeth showed.
I have prepared our food. The peppers are sweet
and the butter is fresh from the morning.
Yawning and removing the sleep from her eyes,
she confronted the aroma of slightly burnt vegetables.
He raised the silver cutter at her
(her lip gloss twinkling
in the reflection of the blade)
and gave her the peppers and the butter.

As Letty Saw It

Harold is adorable but horribly lost.
I'm sympathetic to his flamboyant
murder-mystery criticism
and frequent complaints about the blank factory
where he toils on a work line
correcting the faults of steel gates.
I think it's great when he rants and shouts
about the crumbling and wilting and dying
of the state of short fiction, but the fact is
he's unimaginative and second rate.

Think of connecting little wires all day,
fixing others' tedious mistakes.
You've got to be gentle with a man who looks at metal
from five to eight. You've got to be careful
not to provoke the hate

out of a dull, glazed, thumblike head
when it's been concentrating on wires'the color of lead
the way a saint concentrates
on not taking someone to bed
until it's too late. I like Harold,
but what he says is critical,
and mostly he just stares into space.

Me? I like the sea. Once, on my father's yacht,
we took a trip south to hardly a dot
of an island just off the Red Sea Straits.
Tom was very nice to me, but Harold
didn't say a word the whole damn trip,
just stared into Tom's face with his lower lip
weighed down by the thought of Tom's gorgeousness,
drooling a little, shaking out of pure entrancement.
I always knew Harold had a thing for my Tommy Lance, but

this time it was different. I wanted to throw him over deck.
On the second day, after Tommy had cooked a gourmet set
of sweet peppers and strawberry crepes,
after he sat quietly while I ate,
just as I was about to give him a kiss,
Harold barged in, the jealousy about to fly out.
But thinking of his little metal gates
he stopped, sniffed, nodded and picked
the silver familiar out of Tom's clutched hand,
and, satisfied, smiled and walked out.

As Tom Saw It

I enjoy laundry a lot. I like
to remove the spots and press
creases in the suits. I've had a challenge or two.
One was a blue dress of Letty's,
just before we started going out. I was uncomfortable
with her being rich. But I gave it a shot.

When I got the stain out I told her the news.
She, finding me attractive, accepted a date.
Believe it or not, we fell in love.
She told me it was fate. And though
I didn't understand, I was content
to walk hand in hand with such grace.
I bought a TV to feel a little richer
and thought of expensive things. I think it worked.

My favorite was the trip on Letty's father's yacht.
It was so nice to float in the ocean.
Honestly, I'd never been on a boat.
Harold knew how it worked, so I just cooked
my mother's old recipes, some of which I burnt.
But it was fun, the crepes were a good bite,
and *it's not how well you did it but whatcha learnt...*
That's what my mother used to say, looking like a chef,
inserting her best knife into a chicken's front.

If I remember right, the day of the second night
was the day I fixed the strawberry crepes.
A funny thing happened. Harold got hungry
having smelt the food, but Letty and I ate it all.
So when he came into the sleeper room
he found it empty and couldn't wait.

You should have seen the smile on his face.
He walked over to where we sat,
clapped the butter knife from my hand and stole our plates
to the other room to scrape
the dishes where the scraps were left.
I laughed and laughed.

I really like the sea, the way the waves
are blue when they are not green, and I like
the birds over it, the way
they are.

SCULLY'S FATHER IN SPACE

Scully lost his dump truck
in the sand behind
the rose bush.

His father left his mother
at the BBQ house in June,
saying he was going to the bathroom.

Scully's got a haircut,
and dad's on the way
to the moon.

Dad's mean when mom's scared,
but now he's left
the atmosphere.

Mom loves her son
too much. Her touch
is in the alphabet,

it's in the soup and afternoon.
Scully lost his dump truck,
and dad's on the way to the moon.

Mom's trying to catch a man,
but has no luck. She drives
a Chevy pickup truck.

Scully likes to be afraid.
He likes to hide behind the lamp.
He likes to smile to know he can.

Now that Scully's nearly seven,
who will take his mom to heaven?
Dad will want to tear him up.

But dad's an astronaut, he's happy
picking pieces of rock,
floating around,

looking at the swirl of dust
and sea, looking through clouds,
looking for Scully,

about whom, from so
far away, he is
said so much to care.

LONG DIVISION

The desk fills with
white sheets. He shapes them
into airplanes. His mom's

away for awhile, not long.
Ms. Laury will teach him
right and wrong. "You've got to

divide by four and
bring down one."
When Ms. Laury talks

he tries to think
what she wants.
She sends him along.

The principal says,
"make an adjustment,
screw your cap on."

Mother's letter reads,
Seriously, Benny,
anytime you want.

She writes him to say
she needs this.
One day in summer,

he waves to his father
from the glass square
of an airplane window.

Too many factors.
Each move he makes
makes a zero.

WALK HOME

After the bells,
Angela crosses the white zone with Mike,
her blond hands
pressing her skirt down. If it lifts

I'll forget my tables.
In math I'd been staring at the back of her head
when she turned around and said
stop staring. Across the street,

a circle forms where Lance Chambers laughs
with his opponent in a bush.
Lance would like to fight me,
and so would Roger.

School fades into a small,
ridiculous dot. Home will be
stepbrothers, mother
in a picture, homework. Pink chalk crosses a

yellow line in the sidewalk
and I think fractions,
not hopscotch. I'm half here, half
somewhere. What's safe is this
time between two buildings.

THE DUST TREE

You see something you recognize
in the half-erased
flecks and curves

of print, the night-green
blackboard. Jimmy
touches your hair

and you can't remember
the word *quit*
so you let him,

while the teacher
writes more, explains
more. She flashes

three times four, six times two.
Between her teeth the numbers
slip into pattern,

and what she means you know
is what you can't say
or understand. Her tall hair

shocks the boy in the corner
who's been saying
any answer.

Math is a code
of equivalents.
All lies.

In Spring,
sudden rushes of rain
and tornado watches

late in afternoon.
Skies darken as homeroom
empties and halls

fill with every grade.
Time to think again
of the tree

on the walk home. How
its musty green leaves
and oval shape

are full of tiny,
hidden birds.
Your room at home

is safe. At night
you'll remember snow
coloring trees

and the language spoken
when the territory
wasn't yours.

TODAY IS A GOOD DAY FOR BEATING UP ROGER

The clock slides its hand around the white as Roger
smoothes his foot towards Samantha
and gives me a look. She leans back and mouths
sorry. When he breathes he slurps.

In Geography we have to think till three. The equator
bends around the earth and heat gathers around the Canary Islands.
Latitude measures with ninety degrees.
Longitude, thin red lines on Roger's long-sleeved shirt.

Toads are going extinct in Barranquilla.
She's in love with him, though we're only twelve.
Mrs. Billington passes photographs — Endangered South
        American Amphibians.
Three arms, two tongues, no eyes, a blue toad with a horn in its
        mouth

attached in reverse. Toads, she says, are not that different
from humans. Roger makes a face like
purple jelly in a jar, pointing to the vivarium,
where Santa Claus, the class bullfrog, has died of boredom.

Mrs. Billington explains Global Warming and says
many of the things now living will soon be dead.
Bells shatter the classroom. Time to fight Roger.
At the end of a block a circle gathers. We stand two feet apart.

A NIGHTTIME SEARCH FOR CROCODILES

This evening we will be searching for crocodiles
in the marsh. We would like to see some mating,
but it's not the season. The tackle light brightens
the periphery, all we will need to see.
We are equipped with mosquito net, tangerines, a tank
of water and batteries for the flashlight.
Now take your right hand and let me know
if there's a bulb down under the heat lamp.
If there's a bulb down under the heat lamp
we'll be all right for several hours,
if not all night. It does get cold out
among the slippery hills of peat, drifting
toward the open mouth where the river starts.
Only we won't go that way, or that far.
If you begin to miss your home or remember
what you forgot, remember, we don't have a radio.
We don't have a can of soup or a burner to heat supper.
If we get tangled in the rough of branches
where the saw grass conflates and the bullfrog
blows out its throat, don't be alarmed.

NINE FATHERS

My real father disappeared
in the third year
on a balloon ride
at the April fair. The hot air

lifted him high above
the tiny cities. Mother said
she made him mad. She said it was
her fault, mostly.

My second father
was a coal miner.
He came back black
from the narrow hole.

Above the cave
there was a jagged cloud.
Mother wept in the summer yard
between the poles.

My third father
was a captain in the Navy.
He had an anchor on his shoulder,
a bullet in his toe.

He lost his forearm in Penom Penh.
He said the anchor was a scar of woe
and showed us how it felt
hard against the chin.

My fourth father lived in jail.
He was safe behind the window.
Mother whispered on the phone.
She said she liked to spend

time alone. She thought
she had him caught.
He got out on parole.
My fifth father

was his lawyer.
He took us in the colored plane
and rolled over in reverse.
We wrote a letter on the sky.

On a mountain rock
my fifth father broke.
A hired crew
picked the pieces up.

My sixth father taught me how to
tie a tie and wish for luck.
Do it like this, he said. How?
Like this, he said. Oh.

His body bobbed
beside the placid ducks.
Like fish,
they dragged him from the water.

My seventh father was deaf and blind.
My eighth was a film star with a silver gun.
Under mother's sweater,
he shook it side to side.

When mother grew old, my first father
reappeared. He waved, wedged in a tree.
The flat balloon flapped behind.
Mother couldn't breathe. I held her hand.

CASSINI DIVISION

Nine hundred light-years distant
we see rings shadowing the equator, particles of ice, thin bands
or curves. Small swirls of gas feed the rotation of larger eddies,
generating winds up to eighteen hundred kilometers per hour.

The average temperature is minus one hundred eighty degrees.
Helium drizzles down through layered hydrogen, heating as it
falls through the liquid core. Time continues,
and the circles it makes grow wider,

the dark gaps between them becoming more.

DEAR LETTY,

After you were gone,
I sat one night in the backyard.
The metal spike that kept
the flamingo straight
for the last twenty years
was bent. Its mouth
faced the dirt. Plastic wings
drooped like flags
on a still day, white pods
of the magnolias
glowing like closer stars.

I've sold our white fence
and the wooden house on stilts
that the fence surrounds.
I have given away
furniture from the patio: the pink
three-legged chair,
the green rectangular settee, and all
that was comfortable inside.
Walls have been scrubbed twice
and hardwood floors,
relieved of weight, shine.

The monkey grass,
which made the walk

to the doorstep green,
is dry as clippings
of old hair and brown
as the dirt it will become.
Letty, the stars are falling now — so many.
I have loved you for as many years
as there are wrinkles around my eyes.
Don't think I will stop
growing wrinkles there.

FIRST THERE CAME A LETTER

First there came a letter from a tree,
of how the tree had loved you from afar.
Then came a real tree, or part of one,
and the yellow leaves couldn't fit in the yard,
so the men of leaves had to come
and take the tree away.

Third there was starlight
in the bed of a creek. There was no water.
The mouths of the wolves were dry.
Then you came one day to lie there,
and the animals drank
of your kindness, so the star slipped away.

Fifth the sea was full of sails. The birds
were what you were
when you were young. Their black eyes
loved you from the sky. Then the sailors
took you downward below the keel, and the birds
were gone for the distant clouds.

Seventh the land will never cry,
but cries this time,
for you have joined the world.
Autumn is a way the world thanked you.

For a year the yellow petals were never brown,
and nothing of the season ever fell.

Ninth you will never be owned.
No matter what you can't understand,
the wind will never own you.
Through the red days of the scariest years —
even now it is letting you go,
and will always be letting you go.

THE COLOR BIRDS

He would like to stop
becoming what he's not,
and now it's too late.

Look at him,
trying to peek a last time
through windows of people he admires,

stumbling over bricks,
mashing up the grasses.
Lie down! Lie down! the people say.

You are too old for reinvention.
The future you kept like a map
in the glove box

of a sailboat has sailed off.
What is left
is creeping in the bushes

with smelly boots. No more
resting in the collarbones
of people who liked you,

weeping there,
remembering.
Where you are headed

there will be no sunlight
or versions of God.
Nor will there be rain.

And what you think is music
will be the sound of hope
relinquishing itself

out of the pores of your body.
Where you are headed,
the road is unpaved

and is no road. The full wings
have come
to make you empty.

TWELVE TULIPS

Twelve dead tulips are in the mailbox
again. Twelve dead tulips
in the mailbox. Thank you,
I received the flowers you squished
into my mailbox. What is the meaning
of a vanilla-colored tulip?
I have a problem:
a dozen vanilla-colored tulips
squished in my mailbox. I have
another problem, too: someone
has sent me twelve tulips. I think
I've received someone else's mail,
a bouquet of twelve tulips. Listen,
there's something in the mailbox,
and I think you should know
it's twelve tulips. Did I tell you
what I found in the mailbox? *It's not*
twelve vanilla-colored tulips? Yes,
it is.

TEXAS

The nosebleed
of the cottonwood. Land of God.

The land of aluminum siding and food.
I'm from the creek and the deep bayou,

the summer flower and the mockingbird.
Land of endless neighborhood.

Land of good. I'm from the green
grasshopper, the hornet and the dirt-dauber.

The millipede, the centipede, the spider.
The electric bug-snapper.

I'm from Texas. That's Southwest
of Northeast. And a bit to your left.

I'm from the land of the oil pump
and the trash dump,

CB radio
and the tornado.

I'm from the land of "get up and let's go!"
Land of the Superbowl

and Jell-O. Odessa, Kermit and Louisville.
Land of the fall at Wichita

and the dunes below Penwell. The sea shell
of Galveston.

Land of the Pecan
and the Oak,

where the locust
burns in the mulberry

and sings in the scarecrow's eye
and sings in the hull of the lake boat

and the speedboat
and the gin.

Land of the yellow rose
and the Sunday sermon.

Land of the holy water
at Houston.

Land of the cow chip, the corncob and the cornerback.
Land of the clogged-artery heart attack.

Land of the blitz, the stomp and the sack.
Land of the Crockpot

and the astronaut.
Land of the Black-eyed Susan.

And the black eye of the North.
Land of the beer can,

the barbecue, the brave
and the Dairy Queen milk shake.

Land of the warring sexes.
I'm from Texas.

Land of the loan shark.
Land of the handshake.

LAST MINUTE SQUIRREL TRAP

What he hated most
were squirrels in the peach trees.
"Squirrels and birds," he said,
"hate to see themselves, but they
sure like peaches." My grandfather
busied himself with pie tins
strung to branches and sometimes
took me beneath the bird cage
around the side of the house
to show me the honeysuckle
and red azaleas.

Two months before he died,
my father and I went to his house
in the middle of the night.
He had slipped under again
and needed sugar. It was difficult
getting him to sit tall enough
to breathe. There was choking,
laughter, spitting up, pupils
under the lids of his eyes.
A cup of orange juice
brought him back.

One morning he suggested
I attach a long cord

to the door of the cage.
Leverage it on a branch.
Drag the cord and wait on the porch.
Wait to see the squirrel coming.
Watch as it crawls up the trunk
into the branches, into the fruit
that hangs near the empty cage.
When the squirrel enters the heart
of the cage, bring down the door.

LIVE OAK

We sit beside his father's grave, cracking acorns.
I ask my father to tell which oak makes this hull.
He says red oaks are black
and have no acorns.

The plaque reads H.F. FEAGIN 1912-.
His father wouldn't have liked
the death date missing on the plaque.
Don't wait around.

The Live Oak is evergreen.
It divides over knotted roots.
My father points to the top. A warbler
balances in the branches.

GROVE HILL

As I grew older, I would find him wandering out
under horse-apple trees, among the stones.
These stones, inscribed with family names,
made a row of teeth, jagged,
and late at night
you had to be careful not to stumble over tree roots
risen out of soil or on one of the heavy green apples.
I was seeing him already gone.
He knew he was followed as fathers know
the footsteps of their sons. I never said a word,
but coming back into the house,
I left a light on so he could see
as he walked down the hallway
back to bed. He was not a sleepwalker.
But the inward gaze, the hills
down the lanes furrowed into the eyes,
made me think he was alive with a grief wakened
only in dream, and grief
a road in the dark, between the apples.

OLD FAMILY HOME

The new home has a different name
and glass doors. Now she passes
the butter squash, pecan pie,
shifts three generations
of family quilts. *Good morning.*
How we die is similar
to the erosion of houses. Slowly,
the woodwork fails.
The dump truck comes for
glass, pipes, boards. Mirrors,
lamps, the smell of old rooms
are remembered. We hear sounds
of whisking spoons, can recall
voices the house kept from leaving it
or the one it let go into the yard.
In this home we had
our first birthday or last. We saw
the comet pass, its only appearance
in a century. Pecan trees rose and fell.
Pears gathered in metal buckets by the concrete
water faucet, a red basket, fuchsia roses
rising at the front door.

PRELUDE

Some will speak
in sounds you understand.
Other sounds will pass you by,

you cannot catch them.
It will all change, if you don't like them,
it will all change.

Some of the sounds
they make will be sounds
to try and save you.

As you will see,
the end
makes the story.

If any of them come to love you
it only means
they would like to save you

but know they can't.
It will all be easier
if you come

to love them back. Others will say
it's best to keep love
at a distance.

Just stay warm
in the winters
if you can.

You'll see what I mean.
There will be many signs
for everything.

VISITOR B

You've been kind. You've pleased me
and my family. But you must have been
older, quieter, more full of life. No,
I don't remember you or your photographs.
You have brought something white, too,
which I don't remember. I don't recall
your habits, hands or teeth.
You are obsessed with objects. So am I,
but I like the ones I'm obsessed with.
I can't tell if you're angry or sad.
You say you speak to me in my language,
but then why must I suffer those squeaks.
You continue to squeak and seem serious.
It is not true what you say about Pluto.
Pluto is six hundred million miles from here.
I can assure you you've never been there.
Also, what you say about the word
"happiness" is false. What you say about roses
is true, but I've heard it already.
You've got the wrong plane, wrong scenario.
When you hit Y you should have
hit C and multiplied it by X.
It's too cold for you here.
You'd need to grow hair and get a coat.
It's good you tried though, or you would
never have known where you're not from.
Try someone else. Perhaps they'll remember you.

DESIDERATUM

I felt compelled
to know the nature
of what I saw.

Light on bamboo shoots
and winter ivy. I don't know
what was meaningful.

Some days, you laughed and turned red.
Others, ice-burn
drawn inward.

There were trees, lights, hills, roads
and sometimes love,
or love's other,

a grave dementia
I mistook for misery.
At the end,

light throbbed.
I was small compared to
other things and knew little.

LAST

What they said, once.
What they didn't say.
What didn't last, which lasts
always.

What you remembered,
later, harder, further away.
What you asked.
What was lost

and opened. Who was last
to return, to see it
their way, to see
a way.

In the open door,
who laughed. Who
left, and kept leaving.
What you said, once,

which lasted. Which burned.
What you didn't say.
What you didn't ask.
What they didn't hear.

IN THE COOL HOUSE

Leave the others. Leave
the boats in the green water.
It will be June. In the cool house,
sleep under the tree.

Come night the burning candle.
Come day, the opening dream.
Soon, the white of the tree
will reappear.

We are ourselves
in the cool house
of old doors. Mornings,
sunlight in the glass.

Winter snow shifts
over the limbs.
We remember the others' laughter
and are glad.

Yes the white flowers in the vase. Yes
yellow flowers in the bowl.
And the grapefruit and pear.
Dish of new strawberries

in the window. Leave them. Leave
the boats in the black water.
It will be May. In the cool house
dance under the tree.